To Be a Dancer

To Be a Dancer
Canada's National Ballet School

Text by Gloria Varley
Photographs by Peter Varley
Foreword by Erik Bruhn

PETER MARTIN ASSOCIATES LIMITED

Published with the assistance of the Canada Council

Library of Congress Catalog Card Number: 73-145770
ISBN: 0-88778-053-9

Printed in Canada by Herzig Somerville Limited

Peter Martin Associates Limited
17 Inkerman Street
Toronto, Ontario

For Betty Oliphant
with admiration and affection
and for Robert A. Laidlaw
the school's benefactor,
patron, and friend.

The Interviews

The text of this book was compiled from taped interviews with the following people:

VINCENT BLADEN, former Dean of the Faculty of Arts and Science, University of Toronto; Chairman of the Board of Directors, The National Ballet School

JOY BOARDMAN, in charge of The National Ballet School residences

LOIS BOARDMAN, student in Craftsmen's Course, Royal Ballet School, London, England; graduate of The National Ballet School

WILLIAM BOARDMAN, Director of Special Projects, The National Ballet School

KAREN BOWES, principal dancer, National Ballet of Canada; member of the Board of Directors, The National Ballet School; graduate of The National Ballet School

CAROLE CHADWICK, Ballet Administrator and senior ballet teacher, The National Ballet School

ROBERT DESROSIERS, student, The National Ballet School

DAVID GORDON, dancer, Nederlands Dans Theatre; graduate of The National Ballet School

PATRICIA GOSS, art teacher, The National Ballet School

GILLIAN HANNANT, dancer, National Ballet of Canada; graduate of The National Ballet School

ANGELA LEIGH, ballet teacher, Programme in Dance, Faculty of Fine Arts, York University, Toronto; former ballet teacher, The National Ballet School; former principal dancer, National Ballet of Canada

STEPHANIE LEIGH, dancer, National Ballet of Canada; graduate of The National Ballet School

BETTY OLIPHANT, Director and Principal, The National Ballet School; Associate Director, National Ballet of Canada

THE HONOURABLE MR. JUSTICE JOHN H. OSLER, Supreme Court of Ontario; Past President, The National Ballet School; member of the Board of Directors, The National Ballet School

LUCY POTTS, Vice-Principal (Academic), The National Ballet School

WENDY REISER, graduate student, The National Ballet School

TIM SPAIN, dancer and choreographer, National Ballet of Canada; graduate of The National Ballet School

VERONICA TENNANT, ballerina, National Ballet of Canada; member of the Board of Directors, National Ballet Guild of Canada; graduate of the National Ballet School

Veronica Tennant

We came to Canada in 1955 when I was nine and I went immediately, luckily, to Betty Oliphant who had her own school on Sherbourne Street. During that time I was going to Bishop Strachan and taking my ballet classes. It was getting impossible, absolutely impossible. After school I'd rush off to my ballet class—I had one every night—and then come home about ten, have dinner, and start my homework. It was really ridiculous. The only answer for anyone who seriously wants to be a ballet dancer is to go to a school that can combine the two. There were really sad cases before of girls who had to leave high school at fourteen or fifteen because they couldn't keep up both.

I always did want to be a dancer. I started when I was four and I took to it like a fish takes to water. In England, the school I went to had ballet as part of the curriculum. And yet I still had a natural sort of childhood where I'd read a book about a doctor, and I was going to be a doctor, or I'd read a book about an actress and I was going to be an actress. But underneath all that I was somehow going to be a dancer as well!

I used to regret not going to university. I don't now. I did have the knowledge that I could get high marks and that I would be able to do other things in the world if I had to. Now I know it would have been bad for me to do anything else but dance because everyone has to use whatever his biggest talent is. It's a tragic thing, it's a crime, if you don't. I might have been able to be many other things but none of them would have been as good. I don't ever regret deciding as I did.

I had had friends outside the school, but it was hard to keep them up because all of a sudden life seemed so different. I always try to escape the word dedication because I find it hackneyed and over-used, but you really do have this dedication to something. You knew what you were working for and you became much more independent and more self-reliant than your contemporaries who went to other schools.

1

Angela Leigh

My training was totally different because I was living in London (England) and I had to go to special ballet classes all the time, and I had to do my school work separately. I took two or three classes a week after the first year or so, and that was quite a lot in those days. I think I stopped formal school when I was about fourteen. I was then living just outside London, and it was during the war, and everything was totally chaotic.

So when I was fourteen I started to go to what is now the Royal Ballet School, and there I went into daily training similar to the kind of thing they're getting at the school now but without the academic. They didn't start the academic until after the war. I wasn't fortunate enough to have the two things happening together.

I left the school and went into a review up in Blackpool. It was a success up there so they decided to bring it into London and I was doing twice daily shows for about a year. After that I got married—I got married very young—and came to Canada, and I started my own school up in Orillia. I was nineteen when I started that school, and when it got to be fairly successful I moved over to Barrie and had a school in Barrie too a couple of times a week.

After I'd been teaching about three years, Celia Franca came out. I dropped everything at that point. I can remember coming in for her classes—she gave a class every Sunday—and then she started forming the company. I think I was one of the first seven to be asked to join. I was with the company about fifteen years.

Stephanie, my daughter, never seemed to have quite the same kind of drive for it that I had, when she was little, but I started her taking classes with Betty and she liked it. She decided herself that she wanted to go to the ballet school, and she was the youngest pupil there when it first opened. She was ten.

Stephanie Leigh

I loved the school. I liked it when it first started, when it was so small and there were only two of us in grade six. We had a ball.

I was very loud—I used to sing in the dressing room and they could hear me throughout the whole school. Then Miranda and I used to sit in the lockers. We'd get right in to eat our lunch, and close the doors, and they'd never know where we were. They'd say, "Now where is Stephanie?" And I'd be sitting in the locker looking at the teachers, and they couldn't see. I can't even half get in one now! We used to fold our legs up and close the doors and talk through the holes. If Miranda and I weren't together we were very quiet. But when we got together! Climbing through the windows and things like that. I got in a lot of trouble when I was young. It was fun though. It was really good.

John Osler

Almost from the moment I was made a member of the Board of the Ballet Guild, I was asked to form part of a committee and pretty soon, as chairman of the committee, to investigate the possibility of setting up a school. In fact, at the first annual meeting I attended, I remember being most impressed by Miss Franca's report and the very large proportion of it devoted to the feeling that if this ballet company was ever going to amount to what it should, it would have to be supported by a school. It all sounded like a pipe dream at the time. In the matter of a few months I found I was involved in trying to find out whether it was possible.

Well the first thing I did was to sit down with Betty Oliphant and with Celia and with Carmen Guild, who was then the manager of the Guild, and work out a few estimates of what sort of costs we might be talking about, how large a number of children we could handle, and just how the academic side was going to be looked after. Sort of a preliminary survey of the nuts and bolts side of the operation, because Betty and Celia knew perfectly well what they thought of the artistic side and what their aims were. What we were trying to do was examine the practicality of what was obviously a desirable aim from the artistic point of view. None of us I think knew much, if anything, about running a school. We pretty well had to start from scratch.

Some of our estimates of course were wildly under what actually proved to be necessary, but we optimistically came to the conclusion fairly soon that the thing should be feasible and that we would recommend it for some time when there might be, if not a surplus, at least a small enough deficit to make it look as if it might be possible. Jumping ahead a little bit, we very soon got to the point where we had to start looking around for properties and trying to work out what kind of a property might be acceptable. We were thinking mostly in terms of large abandoned residences, abandoned in the sense that the district might have become non-residential leaving a few white elephants that we might adopt. A good many people were looking around for places of this kind but the person who perhaps looked more energetically than anyone else and who ultimately found the old church, which was the first building we bought, was Elsie Agnew, Mrs. Herbert Agnew, who deserves great credit for the vision she had of what could be made of the building. It was a Quaker church originally and we bought it from a Baptist sect. I'm not sure what branch it was. It was a sort of subdivision of the Baptists, and the principal feature of the ground floor of this church was a very large pool they used for their rituals, which we had to get rid of to start with before we could open up the floor. They also had a sloping auditorium, the church floor was sloped down to this pool idea, so that we couldn't make use of that. We had to lay new floor entirely.

Well then it was the usual story after they started alterations. The mess was indescribable. Of course there was a great deal of clearing out and destruction to be done at first and we were wondering whether it was ever going to work out, and then of course the question arose of whether we were going to get it done within the time. I think it was a week late and there was still a lot of work going on at that time, but we did open within a reasonable time of

the date we promised the parents. I think you can say that Betty Oliphant, Hilda Bennett and I have been in one way or another connected with the thing right from the word go. At first Mrs. Bennet did everything. She was Betty's assistant; she was the school administrator; she was counsellor to the girls; she was liaison with the parents; she was, I hesitate to say girl Friday because she was already a mature woman, but it was that sort of job that she did. She was the bridge between the artistic world and the business world. She'd had some experience in both. She was very good at explaining them to each other and pacifying people.

Betty Oliphant

Bob Laidlaw is our great patron and friend. The school really depends on him. He was always interested in the company and so when the school started he became interested in that too, right from the beginning. He's marvelous to the children. He gives them Christmas presents, usually beautiful art books, and every year he gives a big, big party for the graduates. The children all love him. They made him the most gorgeous Christmas card because that's what he likes best, something they've done themselves. And then there's the building fund, and scholarships, and landscaping—his financial help has been absolutely tremendous.

But it is really as a friend that we hold the warmest thoughts of him. We're very lucky that his love of ballet and affection for children brought him to us in the first place and that he has remained such a wonderful friend to all of us.

Another person who's been invaluable is David Higginbotham. He was our first treasurer—initially he volunteered for just one year but then stayed on for several more. After that he became vice-president and then, in 1970, president. Having this sort of continuity in the people who've helped organize the school has been a tremendous advantage.

John Osler

Another memorable day Betty and I spent in my office, and in the course of an afternoon we picked the whole academic staff. We had advertised and then we'd made appointments for the full half day for interviews and we saw a wild variety of people. I suppose we saw about thirty people in the course of that afternoon. Some were youngish girls from more isolated parts of the country who had always felt they might do something different, and they had either minimum qualifications as teachers or no qualifications as teachers at all but simply thought that something connected with the arts was the sort of thing they wanted to do. We had about six of those who we had to be very polite to and not communicate with any more, and then about three people who really turned out to be quite excellent. Mrs. Haworth was a first class person and she was put in charge immediately of the academic side, subject to Betty's general direction. She was a qualified teacher who had also been connected with the arts. She ran some sort of dramatic organization in Bermuda for some time and she had radio experience as well as teaching experience. She'd been head of the classics and English departments in a large girls' school in Toronto and she was perhaps feeling that the time had come when she wanted a lighter work load. I don't think she realized, and certainly we didn't, the job she was going to have getting the school going under our auspices. She was a tower of strength for the first few years.

We were really extremely lucky that day because we also came to an arrangement with Lucy Potts, who is now the academic vice-principal. We were tremendously impressed with her actual qualifications. Her native language originally was Russian. She speaks French fluently. Right from the start she undertook to organize the French programme which is, I think, most successful.

I think we thought in terms of fifty to sixty as the sort of optimum at that time and quite early we began to realize the very skillfull way in which Betty persuaded the Board that an ever-expanding policy was the only one that was ever going to work. She has a sort of step-by-step technique which is probably the one every really successful principal has adopted. She would tell the Board from time to time when things became absolutely imperative. She never encouraged negative discussion. In other words, there was never a time in the early days when we really seriously looked at anything at all comparable to the size of the operation we have now. It was a question of repairs to an additional room for another makeshift studio and then after that the possibility of perhaps acquiring an additional building on the street as it became vacant. One by one she'd disclose some of the thoughts that she had and we would do them one by one and then of course we woke up after a while to find that we were really committed to quite a large undertaking. But it's proved possible by this step-by-step method.

Robert Desrosiers

Her ballet teacher asked my sister if I wanted to take classes and I said, "Why not? I'll try." And after, my ballet teacher who knew the school and Miss Oliphant and everything—I think I was first asked about coming to the school when I was around ten years old, and my parents wouldn't let me because they thought I was too young then. Later I was twelve or thirteen and I had an audition at the Place des Arts. That's when I came.

Tim Spain

Actually, my parents wanted me to go to the school. I didn't want to go. I'd started dancing before that, about a year or two before, when my sister had been taking dancing lessons and I'd gone too. And then the Bolshoi Ballet came to Toronto and they did something called *Ballet School* which traced the training process of a dancer, so they wanted young kids to show the first steps. During the time I was working for that, there were a lot of people from the ballet school in the thing, so my parents found out about the school and got interested in it and decided they wanted me to go there, so they sent me. That's how it happened. I was halfway through grade eight when I came. Of course, to go from a regular public school is a big adjustment to make but it wasn't difficult. I hadn't been getting along very well at my other school. I was really glad for the change—a great change too.

Gillian Hannant

I was born in Bermuda, but I came here when I was two, which was fifteen years ago. And for as long as I can remember I've always wanted to dance. There were five children and we could never afford to send any of us to a specialized school, but I nagged my mother for literally years to send me to a ballet school. I was in public school, in grade four. I was nine then, and I was bored with school. So my mother called Anna Haworth, who used to be her teacher in Bermuda—Mrs. Haworth was the academic principal of the school at that time—and she said, "Well, why don't you send her along to our school? She'll have good academic training and she'll also be able to start ballet." So I went. I skipped grade five to go into the school, and I skipped grade eight too. I went from six to twelve and I graduated in 1967, so I'm an old-timer. I've seen the school change. Every time you go back, the school has changed. Not only the physical appearance, but of course the people and teachers. And it's expanded and expanded. It's been fascinating.

Joy Boardman

The beginning? We had come in from Calgary and brought a little boy with us. His parents had been friends of ours for years and he was quite talented, but his mother didn't want him to go into residence. Our daughter Lois had been accepted into the school, so we brought Terry along and he lived with us. But he was rather timid about going away to Montreal to perform in *Nutcracker*. Miss Oliphant had already said Lois would be in it, and she'd be going with him, but he kept asking me. "Aren't you going too?" and I said, "No, but you'll be all right."

I don't know whether Miss Oliphant heard about this or not—I think it just came up in conversation when she called me one day. She said, just sort of casually, "Would you be willing to go along with the children as chaperone?" I said, "Oh yes, I wouldn't mind if you thought it would help." Thinking, you know, that I'd be one of many. Well finally I went down to the office and she said, "There'll be about thirty children you'll be responsible for. Now we may be able to give you some help. Maybe you'd like to take one of the ballet teachers with you." Well, I eagerly grasped at this straw because the thought of leaving with over thirty children . . . I'd been used to teaching, but there they're under your direct supervision all the time and you don't have any problem wondering where they are or what they're doing.

Fortunately everything was quite new to the children. The only thing was, I found it very difficult feeding them and transporting them across roads—a big group like that. However, we managed, and the next year it was just automatically taken for granted I would do it. I even learned to make them up, and field all the sorts of crises that came up.

Then my husband, because he got bored with my never being at home, used to come in and help, and then we started taking children who were in *Nutcracker* and couldn't get home. I remember one Christmas we had about six children staying in the house.

Nigel, our son, didn't come into the school until later. Eventually he came too, for the same reason as Bill—that if he couldn't lick 'em, he might as well join them sort of thing. It just snowballed from then on. I came to teach at the school because one of the teachers was going to have a baby. Whatever emergency came up, they used to call me and I used to fill in. They didn't have an assistant matron for one house, so I went in as assistant. Then what happened after that? Oh, they had a chance to buy this house for the boys' residence.

I went to see Miss Oliphant one day, I think it was about Nigel, and we were discussing this and then she said, "You know, we've got a good chance of buying the house next door. How would you like to run the residence for us?" And I said, "Oh sure!", just like that, sarcastically. I thought she was joking too. And then the next thing, the house was bought and I went into her office one day and heard her on the telephone saying, "And I've got just the two people who are going to run it." Then she said to me, "You don't know how grateful I am." Then of course I was so far in I couldn't really refuse. So I went home and told my husband and we discussed it and, well, he likes boys and I like boys . . . .

This is why, really, Bill decided to leave his office job. I wasn't seeing anything of him and he wasn't seeing

anything of me. We were living two separate lives. It's the second year he's been here. He teaches grades five and six and substitutes in the other grades too.

At first the French-speaking students didn't have any special help. Now my husband and I, in addition to everything else, we teach the French children English. Poor Robert had to struggle through on his own, only he did exceptionally well. Before the end of the first year he could speak English very well.

Robert Desrosiers

About speaking English, I was pretty uncomfortable when I first came because I never had such a problem before. In Montreal it never occurred to me that I would have to one day speak English. But when I came here I realized that I needed to learn English. And oh yeah, I can help the others with their French!

Bill Boardman

One way Robert has changed, you couldn't tease him when he first came.

Robert Desrosiers

Well, French humour is different from English humour, so maybe I'd just find what you were saying ridiculous and get mad about it.

Karen Bowes

The first year I was in residence I was in what they call the bunkroom. There were two bunk beds for four girls in one room, and the room wasn't big, but it was adequate. And you know, it was comfortable, but with four children in one room it got to be known as where the black sheep went. Or if you weren't a black sheep, then when you got into the bunkroom you became one! That was fun. We gave our matron a terrible time. She used to come in with a little bell and say, "Lights out, girls", and of course at nine o'clock nobody was ready to turn the lights out, ever. So we did things like putting the bunks together and putting a blanket across. And luckily we had one girl whose parents lived in Willowdale and she could go home weekends. Well, she'd come back with Yorkshire pudding and cakes which she made on the Sunday, and with our candles and cakes we'd put this blanket up and make a picnic after lights out. Which was always a disaster because the matron *always* found out. Somebody one day sat on a cake, and one day an ice cream sundae was shoved into a blanket and remained there the rest of the year.

We did terrible things. We had a storeroom in the basement where the big beautiful Delicious apples were kept, and the cookies that the matron had spent hours making, or the cooks had made. And it was inevitable— we all snuck down and had at least two extra cookies that we weren't supposed to have. We were very naughty, and I think we probably had a few stern talkings-to, but other than that we were pretty much left alone and allowed to be children.

The Christmas parties, they were a big highlight. We could do skits if we wanted to at Christmas, and we'd do terrible takeoffs on the teachers. You know, pull everything out of the closet, everything that bugged us about the teachers, or anything that was funny about them, or each idiosyncracy they had. We'd bring it all out into the open. But that was fun. And for some reason we always ended up, a few kids at least, crying because we had to go away for Christmas.

I'd want children of mine to have the same sort of environment. And I guess that's saying something. It was that good.

I think I probably had more fun being in residence with all those kids than if I were at home, even though I had brothers and sisters. It was difficult being separated from my family. On the other hand, there were so many benefits— it's hard to say which would have been better. I know I've come out of it very happy and I think that's largely due to Miss Oliphant. No matter what problems we had, she always had time for us. And she still does have time. Even now, if I have a problem I can't solve in the company, she always has time to talk it over with me. She's one of the most broad-minded and alive people I know. Especially for someone in her position when she has so much responsibility and so much to take care of.

Even in her teaching, I've noticed that she hasn't set herself a standard and stuck by that standard no matter what. She's continually absorbing things from other people and from other teachers and from other methods, and that, I think, is what makes the school so great. It's not staid. It hasn't steeped itself in a tradition that is dying. She takes the best of whatever she sees and applies it,

assimilates it. She doesn't impose it; she absorbs it somehow, and somehow all those children get the best of everything.

Betty Oliphant

So many people are frightened to send their children to us at ten. This little girl came at ten and the mother kept saying to me, "It doesn't seem right for her to have to grow up so quickly." And I said that as long as it was painless, I thought it was marvelous for her to grow up so quickly.

Most of the kids I know who've been right through the school from age ten to graduation, and are now out in the world, tell me that their relationship with their parents is on the whole much better than it is for their brothers and sisters who stayed home. They have a wonderful time together on holidays. They really appreciate their parents because they've been away from them.

Robert Desrosiers

Living in residence, well, the first year I came I didn't really like it. The first year I was at 506 (Jarvis). I had quite a hard time there, maybe because I didn't know how to speak English yet. But when I came here (Maitland Street) it was pretty good. There's quite a bit of freedom. I think I didn't have too much trouble getting used to residence because we're a big family, so residence life wasn't too bad for me because I was used to noise and sharing things with other people. I was used to that. But I'm sure for some people it's very difficult.

Joy Boardman

It's very hard to have someone come in to residence as a grade eleven student, for instance. Very difficult for them. Some adjust and some don't. The majority of them don't, because they can't stand the little ones being around. They can't stand not being able to go out just when the mood takes them.

David Gordon

I lived in residence for one year. It was a very difficult situation because the boys were then with the juniors on Jarvis Street, all the very young kids, and it was very hard to cope with the problem of making rules for people who were sixteen, seventeen, eighteen and people who were ten, eleven and twelve all at the same time There were three older boys as I remember, and none of us took too well to being supervised a lot anyway. I didn't really live at the residence very much. I stayed there during the week and usually stayed with Tim at his home for the weekends. I guess I'd lived by myself too much for it to be natural for me.

Joy Boardman

I find the children very interesting to talk to. Lots of times they can give you a bit of insight into something. You have to be on their wavelength and take your mind back to how you saw it when you were their age, even though times were different. You have to learn to watch the children and get to know them and then you know, if you watch them, when something is wrong. Sometimes you sense it and sometimes you see it. But I don't think you can take a book of rules and abide by them. We don't have rules, as such, in this house. We just wait and see what comes up. I don't like ringing bells to get them up in the morning or get them to bed at night. All right, so it means a little bit of extra running up and down the stairs, but to them it's worth it. And I don't believe in making a big point of things that to me are not important. I expect little boys to be messy and untidy, and I expect them to go to bed without a wash if they can get away with it. You just yank them back out again.

Carole Chadwick

If I could do it over again, this is the place I'd love to come and be a student. I'm sure there are times when they think, you know, life is hard! And it is—I mean they have long days. Our grade nine students this year take science at ten after eight and it means they have to get up at something like six-thirty in the morning. But then we make their day shorter because of that. They're usually finished by four-thirty and they're not involved in too many rehearsals and things that would keep them late. But they do have a long day and there are lots of pressures on them. You can understand how sometimes they could get fed up.

Vincent Bladen

What you have to know, and what I have now seen particularly with two of my temporarily adopted daughters, is the agony as well as the ecstasy. The agony of the pursuit of excellence. Spiritual agony. Constant dissatisfaction with achievements. It's awfully hard to know what progress you're making. If you're content with mediocrity it's easy. If you're searching for excellence, then there's always the worry. This isn't all dancers, because some of them take life much more easily. But it's probably true of every one who has the potentiality to be a really top star. If they're going to be real artists, they're probably going to have this gnawing agony. I try to offset it, but as I've told these kids so often you've got to be frightened, but not too frightened. Every time I go into a lecture, I'm scared, and I think the first time I go into one not scared will be the time I should quit. But you mustn't be too scared. If you're too scared you can't produce, you can't do anything. If you're not scared at all then you'll probably put on a mediocre performance. I've been reading about Sarah Bernhardt. She was walking past a young woman in the company who was saying in her hearing, "Of course, I've never experienced any stage fright." Sarah turned to her and said, "When you're a good actress, you will."

Joy Boardman

They *are* hard work and they keep you on the run, but you don't have time to get miserable and you don't have time to get bored. You don't have time, period.

They're always hungry, perpetually hungry. I'm always baking. They come into the kitchen and open the 'fridge and say, "Oh, you've got this—can we have some?"

Robert Desrosiers

You made those enormous snacks for us—enormous cakes with jello and whipped cream on top. Those were good.

Joy Boardman

Now with the new house next door, what they plan to do is to have a cafeteria and feed all the children there. And we'll have the little girls living in this house as well as the boys. It just wouldn't be practical to have the big girls! But the boys are disappointed, of course, that we won't be getting the older ones.

Karen Bowes

I think probably the one thing I didn't have when I was at the school was going out on a lot of dates. People said to me, you know, "You probably missed the best years of your life through dedicating yourself to dance." All I could say to that was, in the first place, you don't miss something you don't know about, and in the second place, if you're that interested in doing something that's important to you, it doesn't even enter your mind that you're missing anything. It's a matter of choice and not sacrifice or dedication.

Joy Boardman

Now the boys have their girl friends. And we allow them to have parties. When they want one they come down and say, "Can we have a party on such and such a night?" So then I just call up the girls' homes if they're day students or call up the matron of their residence if they're in residence, and arrange for the boys to pick them up and bring them over here. And they're very good. They clear up the next day. Then they'll come down and say, "Thank you very much, we really enjoyed it." I appreciate that, that they don't take it for granted.

What we do like is for any boy or girl who wishes to date to get a letter from their parents giving permission. A child will say, "Yes, it's all right, my parents won't mind." And then you find the parents do mind. They may feel very strongly. This has worked quite well. I don't

mean that they have to have letters to come over to mixed parties because they're sort of supervised anyway. But to go out on a date, just a couple, to a movie or something, they have to have permission.

Vincent Bladen

I think there's no doubt about it. Betty is much more than a teacher of dancing, though she's a great teacher of dancing. She's a very fine person with extraordinary standards of . . . what shall we say? She's got great integrity, and I think it rubs off. Good people, I think, become better by association with her. That's my feeling. Oh, she makes mistakes! But she's an extraordinary person.

I had a tutor at Oxford and I sometimes wonder why he was such a great tutor. I don't think he ever taught me anything. But he made me feel I could never offer him anything but my best, and how you make people feel like that I don't know. It's partly by being extraordinarily good yourself. It's probably something like that that Betty does to her students.

John Osler

Perhaps the expansionist period really began when Vincent Bladen was interested in the school. He is a remarkable person who has made all sorts of contributions to this country, and the contribution he's made to the school has been second only to Betty's own, I think, because he's taken great interest in detailed administration; he has had access to many sources of funds that we at first had trouble reaching, and his reputation as both an academic person and a person who has done economic research for the government in all sorts of fields has opened doors that have been extremely useful to the school. He's been most generous with his time, and perhaps most important he's been a tremendous optimist. It never occurs to him that we might not get the fantastic sums of money that we need from time to time for various projects and Vincent's inclination has always been to say "Yes" and then go out and get the money or find the people who could do so, and we need an optimist of that kind in this sort of an operation. And I think the fact that we have expanded pretty quickly in the last few years and got away with it is due perhaps more to Vincent than anything else. So it was a great day when he joined the Board and began to take responsibility.

Vincent Bladen

I've just stopped being president—I'd been president for two years. I've probably been around rather more than presidents usually are, partly because I had retired as Dean and was therefore not as active at the university, and I am now partially retired even as a professor.

During the last three years I have taught a class in economics at the school, as a volunteer of course. Then I've been available just simply for advice. Miss Oliphant makes the decisions, she doesn't need much advice, but she needs sort of support and I try to give her that. And I've been involved in helping in discussions with the province and the Canada Council to make sure we were financed.

Then I decided that before I stopped being president I'd like to pay off the debt of the school. Well, this was perhaps overvaunting ambition. However, I talked with one or two people and started on a personal campaign. My idea was to get twenty gifts of ten thousand dollars each. That would pay off our debt. I've never tried to raise money before. I knew it was hard, but I now know it's much harder than I thought. It's just possible I may get it up to one hundred thousand dollars.

The school has not really done much in fund-raising except for its Women's Committee, which was fantastically successful with its Collector's Choice auctions. Now partly, in the early days, they didn't like to go out to get money because they were afraid it would be money taken from the company. I think now the school is so clearly identified as an educational venture that it's possible to go after money for the school and not take it away from the company. Indeed, my letters always said, it is not because I am particularly interested in the ballet that I ask this; I'm interested in the school as one of those institutions that enable children of great talent to develop it to the full within their own country.

I would say, roughly, a resident student probably costs four thousand dollars a year and pays in fees—if paid—two thousand. And I would think that much more than half of them are helped, so we need very big supplements.

On the one hand, nobody can get into the school because they can afford it. If they're not talented it doesn't matter how much they've got. If they say, "Well, we'll pay ten thousand dollars a year," we'll say, "Delighted—we'd love to have the ten thousand dollars, but not your child." On the other hand, we do look into the circumstances of every child and give whatever seems necessary. Normally I would say there's no reason why any child should not come to the school who has talent but who can't afford the fees. They can have the full fee paid if necessary.

Then there's an awful problem. You get a child whose teacher has told the parents how wonderful she is, and she comes to the school and is auditioned and turned down. Then the teacher tells the parents that this is because Betty is Cecchetti instead of R.A.D. (Royal Academy of Dancing) and is just plain prejudiced, and there are long letters explaining that the child is now liable to be ruined for life by this great disappointment.

Then I help to write letters which explain that it isn't whether she's good, or even very good. The question is whether she was better or worse than the one selected for the one place open in the particular grade for which her

age fitted her. In other words, you can't say you've got ten places. You've got ten scattered here, and here, and here, and here. And for each you've got to take a child of a particular age. You may be highly talented, but there may be one who's even more highly talented and there's nothing you can do about it.

You see, you can't take everybody, because our facilities are geared to roughly one hundred and twenty to one hundred and thirty students. If we were to grow beyond that (a) we'd have to have new facilities, a new plant, (b) we'd have to expand the staff, (c) we would lose some of the intimacy the small school has, and (d) we would all the time have a little worry: what is the number of dancers of this type that it's fair to train?

So far there's been no serious disappointments, I think. But they're cutting down the size of the company already. Now it's true our children aren't trained simply for the National Ballet Company. They're trained so that they should be able, and I think are able, to take their place in any first-rate ballet company. in the world. But a lot of them would like to live in Canada. The other companies— I think I'm right in saying this—don't provide the same length of season so that employment with them is less satisfactory. But also, they too are in dire straits. So I think, in all conscience, no one is quite prepared to expand the school.

Another difficulty is that though Betty does do a fantastic job, and gets help in this from the Canada Council, it's impossible to conduct enough auditions across the country. But she was out west last year, and out east this year.

Carole Chadwick

An audition is always rather a difficult time, because we have quite large groups of kids who come. We would have sixty or seventy students, divided into three classes, and out of that we might take twelve. And even there it's only for summer school and then we'll choose after that, and a lot of them are sort of doubtful.

It's very difficult. The parents come to watch and afterwards Mrs. Bennett said she walked in the front door and all the parents were streaming out with children with red eyes. They're so crushed and so disappointed because this is something they want so badly, and they just don't have the physical requirements or something. It's always rather devastating and the parents find it very difficult to understand. Now we do it by letter, but we used to give them, because we didn't have as many, we used to try and say what was wrong with each child. Each child has a sheet to put down comments, and we used to speak to all the parents individually afterwards and say "I'm sorry we can't take your child, because . . . ." This was my task one year and it was heartbreaking, you know, because you'd say to them, well, she just does not have the physique that is necessary, or it's too late. She's fourteen and she hasn't had much training. I finally said, well, this is just our opinion. I mean I'm not saying that she can never be any kind of a dancer, period, but it's just that she doesn't have the requirements necessary for this school. We try to explain and soften the blow as much as we can. We say we are a small school and can only take so many. But the children who are chosen are always elated.

I consciously thought, "Okay, I'd like to do something. What'll I do next?"

Those first things were sort of like the first things that came into my head. I just did it because I thought it was great. But now I'd really like to destroy my mind because every time I have an inspiration, as soon as I let it sit in my head for a while, I cut it up and throw it away; decide it's no good. I imagine myself as an audience watching and I always end up thinking, "That's ridiculous—I wouldn't want to see that." I'd really like to become, in a sense, empty-minded and then just do what I vision . . . vision is a very pedantic word, but just do the things that come. I'm sure I would do well if I could reach that state.

There's another problem I'm having right now. I have so much music which is full of imagery for me, but it's not dance imagery. I have to pull it down to a box with little people in it, and people watching them, and when I pull it down to that then I just have to throw it away. Another problem I'm having with choreography is I find I start doing things arbitrarily because they look all right, sometimes to fill up the music if there's too much music. I really need to work with a composer.

When I do something else it will probably appear to be abstract. In the sense that people use that word when they refer to dance, it means having no story. But at the same time I want people to know what I mean. I want to do something which, even though it appears to be abstract, nobody says to themselves or their neighbour afterwards, "Well, what was it about?" I want to be very explicit, and in order for it to be explicit for each person I have to have a very solid feeling which I don't deviate from. But the biggest thing of all is, you have to work with dancers who want to do it. It's very simply that.

Gillian Hannant

Working with Ann Ditchburn, who choreographed *Listen,* was just tremendous. We did breathing exercises and things that related to the piece she was going to do. She got Garry and I to relax in each other's company because when we first started there was a wall between us and she had to break it down. I was supposed to be blind and he was supposed to be my lover. There had to be something to connect us, I just had to know that he was there, so we did a lot of work and she choreographed it working with us rather than coming in with a piece and showing us the steps. They came out of us, out of all three of us.

Joy Boardman

I think the first performance of *Nutcracker* was the most exciting, probably because the school had never done it before. Now they take it in their stride. Miss Franca took every child individually and coached them for the first *Nutcracker*. I remember we used to go down to the old St. Lawrence Hall with the dusty floors and the mice running all over the place. But the children seemed to like the atmosphere. They enjoyed it.

Lois Boardman

Miss Franca could never find the boys when it came time to do Courtiers. You know the old bell tower? There were stairs going up and you had to be careful where you stepped. It was all rotten and you could go through, but all the boys would go on up there.

Joy Boardman

Then there was the year we went to Vancouver on the train. We were playing charades for hours and hours on end with all the little children. I was absolutely hoarse—I remember that very well. Arriving at two in the morning—it was supposed to have been ten or eleven at at night—and the poor children, we had to wake them up in a hurry and try to dress them. Miss Oliphant met us off the train and she was a bit upset because the girls didn't have their hair tied back. I just said, "You're lucky we got them awake to get them off the train!" One was walking but she was still asleep.

Bill Boardman

Then, coming back, they'd given three performances and a couple of demonstrations so some of them were pretty tired. We were supposed to leave about midnight, so we got to the station and the first thing I heard was my name being paged. I went down and they said, "We're awfully sorry Mr. Boardman, but your coach isn't ready. We're having to change your coach and we're going to put the old colonial style on." Oh my lord! They'd been sitting in the yard for three days. They were damp. No heat. First we had to check we had enough beds to get them all in, then they got it hitched up, but this was about two in the morning.

Then the second night we were chugging along at two or three in the morning—that seems to be our time—when someone started hammering at the door. One of the boys had put his light on, and he blew out the whole coach, the electricity. Everyone was saying, "Be quiet, get back into bed," and the children were saying, "We can't, we can't see." So I went back to check them all over and I couldn't find half of them. Where the beds were there were no bodies. We thought, they can't be very far away. We haven't stopped anywhere. So we started again. Well, we finally got to one—there were five of them in one bed. It looked like opening a can of sardines, heads and tails. We got them all sorted away then.

Remember in Vancouver when they had that Sugarplum party and it turned into a riot? I was supposed to take out the two Claras. They had a candy Sugarplum tree roped off in the entrance, the foyer, and the party was

sort of to meet the cast. Wow! It turned out to be a full stampede. I had to pick the Claras up and carry them away. People pushed right through and broke the tree down. Matrons were snatching things off the children. The Sugarplum tree was really beautiful and it was supposed to be distributed at the end in an organized fashion. But some old lady leaned over and bashed it with her umbrella and that was it. Everyone dove in for the pieces.

Lois Boardman

And there was the time we were on stage and Jeremy Blanton was Master of Ceremonies and then, well, something went wrong and the orchestra played the first twenty-four bars over again for the Courtiers in *Nutcracker*. And we missed it. We stood there, you know— oh, oh! And so Jerry said, "Well, we'll go round again." He was talking to us, directing us, all over the stage. Telling us where to go. All off the top of his head.

It worked. Miss Franca, she couldn't keep a straight face because she thought it was so funny. But we thought, oh we were really frightened because we were young and we thought we were going to get in trouble because we didn't hear. But Jerry just stood there, talking and laughing. "Here we go again, kids. Around again." He really managed it well.

Joy Boardman

Even when shoes come off, the kids have the presence of mind to do something about it naturally on stage. Nobody then told them of these predicaments that can happen. We warn them now, but not then. When you think of how green we were when we first went into it and now, my goodness, we're sure enlightened about a lot of things!

We always encourage the children to watch the performances if they can, and learn all the parts that they can, so you can switch them around. This at first they found difficult. If they were doing Courtiers on one side and they were suddenly changed to the other, this was very hard for them. But now they're quite adaptable and can do it.

The main problem is the parents of children who are in *Nutcracker* for the first time. They *will* roar around backstage wanting to take pictures, and they *will* try to come up into the dressing rooms. You know how small they are, and there's not all that much oxygen when the children are in there. So we had to make this rule that no parents were allowed out of the green room. If they do want to take pictures, we understand, and we send the children down dressed to the green room and they take them there. But one time I had one mother who insisted, and who pushed right past me onto the stage itself between acts to take her child's picture. We had an awful time to get her out of there. As Miss Oliphant has told the children, this is very unprofessional, this sort of behaviour. And it is dreadfully embarrassing to the children.

Betty Oliphant

Now the company's smaller, the school dancers will be augmenting the company much more. And they'll be going into the company, as they used to in the old days, as far more experienced dancers. It's very good for the school.

Veronica Tennant

My first appearance with the company was when I was fifteen. I did black cygnets in *Swan Lake,* the fourth act of the old *Swan Lake.* And then in that year one of the white cygnets fell ill, and I did one of those. The second year when the students were helping out, someone had fallen sick from the first act, so I finally found myself doing all four acts of *Swan Lake.* It was the greatest thrill, and it was also tremendous training. I remember doing that black cygnets, the first thing I ever did. I used to dream about it for weeks afterwards.

Wendy Reiser

The first time I was in *Nutcracker* I was twelve. I was old, really, but it was because I was so short. We went to Vancouver and Montreal and it was a great experience, we had a good time, but it's even better with the company now—I guess because you're getting closer to what you want to do.

Bayaderka, that's a really hard ballet. Coming down the ramp I thought I was going to fall over. All the company girls think it's gruelling too. Most ballets, you get used to them. They say this one is torture every time. I have that to look forward to!

We sent the company a telegram afterwards saying thank you for the experience and the patience and the help and everything. They were really nice. We didn't know what to expect, but it was terrific.

Betty Oliphant

We don't try to influence them at all to join the National Ballet. I think that's up to the company. At the moment, I think that the National Ballet is the best of the companies in Canada. But if the standards of the National Ballet went way down, and the standards of one of the other companies went way up, then I would know that the school dancers wouldn't go to the National Ballet and I wouldn't mind at all. And if, for instance, the National Ballet Company didn't exist—which I would hate very much—then I would want the dancers to go to whichever company was the most suitable to them.

Lucy Potts

The first time she did *La Sylphide,* Nadia was so nervous. But Erik Bruhn was very nice to her. He'd say, "Don't worry, if you forget something I'll tell you." And she found he was also nervous on the stage, so I think they were really hugging each other, he trying to comfort her. He was really considerate. She was very touched the way he did treat her, because you know it was a last-minute thing. Veronica was due to dance and she had her appendix out so Nadia had to step in. She did her first full rehearsal actually on the stage. The performance itself was the first time she'd gone right through the ballet. And Bruhn was very very nice to her. He need not have been, you know, with a young person just being thrown in.

David Gordon

I was surprised. People tend to think I'm a great critic, and to a certain extent I am, but I wasn't here very long before I grew very attached to the company. It has such a fantastic potential. It's not a matter of doing things Canadian. Inevitably if we do things from our own personal points of view which our backgrounds and our social situations have created, we are creating a Canadian style.

Gillian Hannant

In *Kraanerg* rehearsals, it was much different watching something that was only five feet away from you. If you see it on the proscenium stage the effect is much greater. In rehearsals I didn't see all the ballet and I had no real idea of the fantastic patterns he was making. When I saw it on stage it was the patterns of the ballet that interested me. There were some things I didn't like about it. I did like the music and the costumes and the sets. Some of the choreography I found a bit too tumbly, a little bit too acrobatic. But even to do something like that that's acrobatic is a refreshing break from *Nutcracker* and *Swan Lake.*

Although I'd love to do *Swan Lake* corps because it's very strengthening. As far as corps work goes, there's nothing quite as valuable as doing *Swan Lake.* It's so challenging to work with a lot of other people. I mean arms and angles of heads have to be exactly the same, and timing, and lines, and all these things that are so important. But I hear the *Swan Lake* corps is murder on the legs. You have to stand in one position for what seems like hours and the pain is just climbing up your legs, and then you've got to be a beautiful swan and float around. They've cried on stage from the pain. People have said, "I'm going to walk off, I can't stand it." This kind of gripping agony.

I do love working in my bare feet but there's no reason why, in a big company, you can't do small productions that are done in bare feet. And I would like to do modern ballet—in other words, pointe shoes, and a kind of choreography that is based on the straight Cecchetti classical curriculum.

Veronica Tennant

Going into the company, I think if you get a bump at all it's in the second year, not the first year. The first year you're just so enamoured of the whole thing. You go on these awful hideous tours and you couldn't care less. You just love it. You wonder why all the older ones are complaining. The second year is harder. It can be.

One of the things I remember is, I'd do a first performance in something and they'd all come back—Miss Oliphant, Miss Franca, the ballet mistress, the ballet master. That's what I expected. What I didn't really expect was when I'd do something the second or third or fourth time and no one would come back, and no one would tell you how you'd done. At first I thought, "Oh, I must have been terrible." And then I realized that I hadn't been terrible at all. It's just that they're not going to come back every night and tell you how you did. Of course they're there to help you, but they're not there to hold your hand.

I always wanted to go into the National Ballet Company. I'm tempted now to go to other places, but it'll always be to come back to my company, which is here. Probably if this company existed in New York or in London I wouldn't want to go somewhere else, because I would be able to see other dancers all the time and possibly work with them in class. But because we happen to live in Toronto I feel that I have to go away. I'm not complaining. It's just that as a dancer, to grow as much as I want to, I'll have to see more than I'm seeing here.

When I start thinking of going to another company I realize just how much there is here and how really beautifully unique our company is. Although it has not yet made it as a great international company—which I think it will, and deserves to be—I can't honestly think of anywhere I'd rather be than here. You get so much more personal attention and really genuine love than you get in many other companies in the world.

Karen Bowes

I think one of the most devastating things that ever happened to me at the school was when I was in grade twelve and we were writing our final examinations. This was a big onus. Once they were over I'd be free and finished school. I had decided the examinations were so important I would give up ballet classes for that week, so this was my fourth day and I hadn't taken ballet class. It's a very difficult thing to jump into a class, having not taken—the body gets out of shape very quickly.

And then our academic director walked in and said, "Now I have a marvelous treat and surprise for you. Rudolph Nureyev is here to teach you a class!" So I whipped downstairs and threw on my tights and put on my shoes that felt like Dutch clogs. And after an hour and a half of Rudolph Nureyev giving us the hardest class I'd ever had in my life—because I was so out of shape—I think I just collapsed. That was devastating.

We had a lot of people from outside come to give us guest classes. Erik Bruhn taught us, and Ulanova came to teach us a class. And Eugene Valukin, and people from Leningrad. Which was always a big excitement about the school—it's like us having guest artists in the company. Those were good times.

Gillian Hannant

The summer when Madame Eugenia (Farmanyants) came over from Russia, I adored her classes. We had gypsy dances and various kinds of folk dancing, and Hungarian dancing, and ballroom dancing, all character. I just love dancing that way. I guess it's a bit of an ego trip, really, because you can put a lot of yourself in your dancing and you emote. In the gypsy dance it was all shoulders and back and very sensual. Oh, the things she could make us do. She was so alive herself you couldn't be deadpan with her.

Veronica Tennant

Repertoire classes are good, learning ballets that the company does. Every Friday it used to be for us, every Friday night. It was like another little company. They'd make up the whole corps, you see, and the senior students would do the leads. But it's good also to be learning the corps because then if something unforeseen happens in the company they have these senior students who know the roles and they can do them.

Karen Bowes

I went to Russia one summer. A group of seven of us went. We were there for two and one half weeks and we saw a ballet competition, the Fifth International Ballet Competition of Moscow. I was perfectly happy to go as an observer rather than a participant. Competitions are horrible, they really are, to enter. They're just nerve-wracking.

I learned a lot from watching the competition, but as a dancer I find it difficult to watch ballet and not feel left out. I like very much to feel that I can go and do my performance the next day after I've watched one. And to watch for two weeks is extremely difficult. But we were allowed to take classes with the Bolshoi company, which was a great privilege. Miss Oliphant had been there before and she arranged everything for us. If I had gone there by myself or with another girl it would have been impossible.

I was so itchy to get away and study after that. I was going to travel around Europe and see a few more things and I didn't—I went straight to Paris and studied for a month.

Tim Spain

The biggest problem in pas de deux is nervousness. You can't work if you're tense. You have to relax and work. For a girl, it's very close to what she does in her normal technique classes, but for a boy it's a totally different thing. Basically, he doesn't do any dancing in pas de deux, but just learns how to control the balance of his partner and things like that.

You really discover very, very quickly that you can't do lifts with brute strength, and that even if you could it would take away from the quality of the dancing. What you do when you're doing lifts, you pick up the rhythm of the girl you're dancing with, you catch her rhythm. For instance, if you're going to do a lift, you push as she's jumping. You just discover the right moment when it has to go, and this requires being completely relaxed. It takes a little time, but you discover how to relax while you're doing it, and then you find you can pick up the rhythm, and then it gets easier and easier.

Angela Leigh

I give the advanced class ten minutes of yoga in the morning before they start, to get them calmed down and relaxed a bit, and then they can put their minds where they should be. They really come rushing into class and they're all tense from getting changed. So I started this yoga and I think it's having quite a beneficial effect. I've done some very basic exercises with them so far. I mean

I myself haven't gone too deeply into yoga for me to teach past very basic stuff. But it's getting their minds to centre themselves and get into a balanced state, and then they can work ten times as well. They get to feeling their breathing and they start to be more aware of the actual working of the body. The training, the actual technique, is such that it's imposed from the outside, and the kind of things that yoga is trying to teach is something inside, to bring it out. I think a lot of dancers are more aware of the appearance, what it's going to look like, to begin with and then they gradually work in as they develop. That's what I think yoga helps to produce, so that in a sense they're not conforming anymore. They're conforming in that they acquire a certain technique, but they also have to get that other side going to balance it out. Then it all becomes more spontaneous, less calculated.

I'm starting some choreography myself to the *Goldberg Variations* of Bach, and then I'm going to have them do one of the *Variations,* each do a different interpretation, and try to get them into the creative aspect of dance. I think that's probably the next step: that everyone dances, choreographs, teaches, does the whole thing, so they won't be stuck in little grooves—one thing or the other.

I dropped ballet—I dropped the whole life—about three or four years ago and tried to extend the view a little bit, and that's what I'm trying to get through to the kids I'm working with. Trying to enlarge their view throughout their whole life.

Tim Spain

I think the idea of yoga classes is very, very good. You can create a calmness throughout the whole body and a relaxation which makes it possible to work muscularly later on. So often it's easy to go into a ballet class and not be able to work in a muscular way, but in a nervous way—I'm opposing nervous and muscular. But if you begin with the middle, the centre, the inside of your torso and your hips, and you start with breathing, then you can work out, and then you get down to your legs and your feet and the ends of your arms and your head.

I used to think I'll just do what I want to do and I'll get the breath from somewhere, and of course this was a negation of my own body. It was not working with the fact that one of the main sources of rhythm that the body has is breath, which is vital to dancing. We breathe unconsciously and so what you must do is learn again how to breathe, and learn why you breathe and how to use breathing. Make it conscious. And then you let it become unconscious again, but only after you understand it and know it.

Vincent Bladen

I suppose one of the developments of the future ought to be the production in our school of a programme to develop teachers of dance, not of ballet, of dance, for the schools. I think dancing along with music ought to be available in all normal schools. Perhaps what we really need to do is to help provide teachers of teachers of dance for the community colleges. But this is the next decade, this is all in the future. Betty has often thought she'd like to work it out, I think, but she's had several other things to think of!

Betty Oliphant

When I tell the Board of Directors I'm unhappy in a way because we educate the children so well, and show them so many aspects of life, and so many directions in which they could go—and also show them fairly honestly the disadvantages of being in ballet, that they certainly aren't trapped—and when I get a little depressed because we've lost some marvelous dancer who's decided to go in for some other career, Vincent Bladen is the one who's always saying to me, "Look, you know it's absolutely essential, and the ones who are really dedicated will stay." Which they do. And in fact the ones who are really good students *and* have this dedication, and have faced all the other sides, and then still choose ballet—it's rather exciting.

I go around spouting that an artist is first of all an educated person, and that doesn't just mean going to school. It does mean activating the mind. I think one reason

kids in this day and age are opposing the people who teach them is because they know their minds aren't being activated. They resent having material given to them, and being told to accept it for what it's worth. They want to argue and they want to discuss and they want to have their opinions respected, even though in a few years they may have completely different opinions.

We allow a lot of freedom. We bring in outside people. We let them be very controversial. We don't let them break up the school and that kind of thing, but we certainly let them speak as freely as they want to.

Sometimes there's grumbling about having to take a science course or an extra language or whatever the requirement may be. But we do work things out very carefully so no student is ever kept from continuing his education past grade twelve because he hasn't got the proper academic background. We find out what's required in his home—whether it's Ontario or another province or outside Canada entirely—and we make sure his grades and subjects will meet the standards. Even if a boy or girl completes training here at the school and then joins a company, he may still after a year or two decide to go back to school and we don't want him to have any problems about this.

I had a girl in grade eight come to me worried about what she should be. She said she loved to dance, wouldn't know what to do if she couldn't dance, but she was really interested in astronomy too. As she was at the school on a scholarship she felt she should decide—that is, that she had a moral responsibility to decide. I told her not to worry about a choice like that now, that the scholarship didn't matter. At that age she should just go ahead and do

her best in all the things that interest her. I don't start talking to them about that kind of decision until grade ten. That's plenty of time. Until then you can't really tell— the kids aren't mature enough to be certain of their future.

Lucy Potts

We try to give them as broad an education as possible. We try to change, we try to keep up with the times. We want them to develop in every respect. We've introduced Spanish, which we didn't have at the beginning, and we now have Russian. Music has become a compulsory subject. We concentrate much more on music and I think this really started about five years ago.

We have a very good relationship with Jarvis Collegiate. Our students go there for science and they like having them. They say they'll often set the trend in a class. In grade nine, they all go to science. In grade ten, some go. We used to make it compulsory in grade ten, but now we've introduced some other options and made music compulsory. The first year gives them an idea of whether they would like to do science or not. The options are gone into very thoroughly. If they're university material they must have the options which would allow them to go to university should they not want to dance. Nadia is going to go to university now—her husband is working on his music degree so they've decided to go together—but I think she'll come back to dancing or to teaching after that.

Even if they feel that the only thing they want is to dance, at the time, we still have to see that they have the right

options. I explain it to them and they're always very interested. And if they want to choose one subject and we feel that's really not the right subject for them, we have a personal interview and try to make them understand that *this* subject would really be much better for them than the other one, because we know them so well. We know what they're able to do. We know what they're capable of. Now, for instance, Russian. They have to be good language students because it is hard work and it is difficult. Russian they find interesting mainly, they say, because it's so different from any other language. Very seldom do they say because it has any connection with ballet. They just like the Russian for its sake. They often prefer it to French—I teach French and Russian—and some of them like the Russian better than French, which is funny.

Now those who would find it difficult to get into university, we give a very enriched course and not so highly academic. Instead of maths they'll take art; they'll concentrate on theatre arts, on languages if they want to, and we've found that this has worked very well. They found it difficult at first to accept, but I said, "Look, why can't you develop the talents you have? I mean you can do this so much better than other people who are going to university, so why don't you want to develop that? You're lucky that you have this, develop it to the full." So I think they have accepted it very well now.

Patricia Goss

When I first went to the school, the art course wasn't related enough to ballet and to music. You know, the ballet was one thing and the academic work was another, and I gradually tried to get it so that we do things which relate to ballet as well. In fact, right now Miss Leigh has got two of the art students in grade twelve doing costumes —designing costumes and batiking some of them—and then they're also making up the costumes for the choreographic workshop. There's much more of a feeling now of trying to relate the ballet and the art and the music. And to a certain extent we try to relate the history of art course to what we're doing in the art programme. For instance, if the history of art teacher is dealing with a period where she's concentrating on some sculpture, then we would get into the figure and do quite a bit of life drawing. And then we might go into wire figures and some plaster work. Then she was dealing with mosaics at one point, so we did mosaics. Stained glass in churches, we did stained glass at the same time.

In the ballet school we're usually rather short of money so I do my best to scrounge around for anything that anybody's got that they don't want, and I found a very fine stained glass window artist who I heard was throwing away his odd scraps. It's terribly expensive, so I went down to see him and he gave me boxes of gorgeous stuff. Only small pieces, but we actually used a lot of stained glass, cutting it and making designs on glass. It turned out marvelously, and then from there we went into using stained glass in pieces of sculpture, and covering plaster

figures with stained glass—you name it! Certainly in the art programme we do experiment an awful lot.

If you're going to teach art well at all you have to watch for individual style in each personality, and not direct it and say, "I like a bold style" or, "I like a sensitive style" or, "Why don't you work this way?", but really try to bring out individually what each child has got. So after you've got the class motivated, you get out of the way as much as you can and if you feel a child doesn't want you there, then don't even go to see what he's doing. If I feel they do need help and do want advice, then I usually try to throw it back on them as much as possible and say, "Well, what do you think? I could tell you what I think, but it isn't my piece of work. You're the artist. It's what you're going to do with it." And as soon as you can give them the feeling that what they are doing is very important, that you value it, then they're well away because you've given them confidence and you can almost see them feeling theif integrity and then they start to develop.

I enjoyed the other school I worked at very much indeed, but this school as far as I'm concerned is absolutely ideal. I have an attic, which to me is just perfect for an art room anyway. It's at the top of this old house, it's all by itself, and I don't think it matters too much how dirty it gets. I don't think anybody minds, because we really do keep it in a perpetual state of muddle. There's so much going on all the time. People come in during the lunch hour or they come up just occasionally because they like being up there, and they do the odd thing on their own whether I'm there or not, and it's a lovely atmosphere. I just love that room. You walk in and it envelops you.

Art should really involve your whole life. A lot of the kids who are now in the company, I meet them on the street and they'll say, "Oh, I'm having an absolute ball. I've decorated our apartment. I've done one whole wall and painted all over it," or "I've done a batik and it's hanging up." This I find terribly exciting.

Carole Chadwick

The Ballet Division has classes after school for amateurs. Anyone can come, they don't have to be auditioned—that is, beginners. Children who have been to other schools, we audition only from the point of view of finding out what class to put them in. We have talked about auditioning everybody, even brand new beginners, but that would draw it down to such a fine line that at the moment we're not doing that, we're just taking anyone.

We take them starting at six and they have pre-ballet, not any sort of formal training. We give them running and jumping and moving with the music and basic positions, and then at seven they start more formal ballet training. I'm not sure how many students we have this year—it's usually about two hundred and fifty to three hundred. We have classes every day from about four-thirty, mostly taught by the regular staff, though we have to augment them with other people who have trained in the school. Then we have classes all day Saturday from nine until four-thirty in two studios. It's a good thing. I still approve completely of proper basic training for children whether or not they're going to be dancers. It doesn't make any difference to me. A good plié is a good plié and I think they should learn it that way. Otherwise they can injure themselves and damage their legs. But

Lucy Potts

It was very exciting when Nadia got in the company. I
try not to be a ballet mother, that's one thing in my life,
I mustn't be a ballet mother like they used to be! Well,
I wanted to see her perform, naturally, as much as possible,
but not to make myself too obvious around the place. Of
course I came to see the others also. I'm always terribly
interested to see all the students I've taught when they're
dancing, so I find I have to see the ballets several times to
appreciate each one, because I can't look at everybody at
once. I really do like to see how they've developed, and
I take just as much interest in their ballet careers as I did
at school when I was teaching them their academic
subjects.

Nadia benefitted by the school in every respect. I mean
some people have asked me, "Well look, if she never dances
do you think she's wasted her time going to the school?"
My answer is no. This will remain with her, five years of
real happiness to carry through her life, and I think this is
what I would like every child to feel, that having been at
the school they have something that perhaps no other
school could have given them.

For further reading

AMBROSE, KAY
The Ballet-Lover's Companion
Alfred A. Knopf, Inc., New York, 1949

AMBROSE, KAY
The Ballet-Lover's Pocket-Book
Alfred A. Knopf, Inc., New York, 1945

BRUHN, ERIK
Dance Perspectives 36: Beyond Technique
Dance Perspectives Foundation, New York, 1968

DE MILLE, AGNES
To a Young Dancer
Atlantic Monthly Press, Boston

KARSAVINA, TAMARA
Classical Ballet: The Flow of Movement
Macmillan Co., New York, 1963

KARSAVINA, TAMARA
Theatre Street
E. P. Dutton and Co., Inc., New York, 1961

KERSLEY, LEO AND SINCLAIR, JANET
A Dictionary of Ballet Terms
Pitman Publishing Corp., New York, 1964

NOVERRE, JEAN GEORGES
Letters on Dancing and Ballets
Dance Horizons, Inc., New York, 1803

The Graduates of the National Ballet School

YOLANDE AUGER, Sainte-Foy, Quebec: 1969 graduate; 1969 to 1971, postgraduate student, The National Ballet School, and *Prologue to the Performing Arts

FRANK AUGUSTYN, Hamilton, Ontario: 1970 graduate; to National Ballet of Canada

JANET BATTYE, Toronto, Ontario: 1963 graduate; to Ryerson Polytechnical Institute, Toronto

VICTORIA BERTRAM, Toronto, Ontario: 1963 graduate; to National Ballet of Canada; now a soloist with that company

FRANCES BICK, Toronto, Ontario: 1968 graduate; 1968 to 1969, Cevenol College, France; 1969 to 1970, York University, Toronto

LOIS BOARDMAN, Toronto, Ontario: 1970 graduate; to Craftsmen's Course, Royal Ballet School, London, England

NIGEL BOARDMAN, Toronto, Ontario: 1968 graduate; 1968 to 1970, postgraduate student, The National Ballet School; 1971 to Ryerson Polytechnical Institute, Toronto

DEBORAH BOWES, Victoria, British Columbia: 1965 graduate; 1965 to 1966, postgraduate student, The National Ballet School, and correspondence courses in mathematics and French

KAREN BOWES, St. Catharines, Ontario: 1965 graduate; 1965 to 1966, postgraduate student, The National Ballet School, and courses in French and Russian; 1966 to National Ballet of Canada; now a principal dancer with that company

GAYLE BOXER, Toronto, Ontario: 1970 graduate; to York University, Toronto

KAY BROWNFIELD, Bradenton, Florida: 1965 graduate; to professional modelling

SUSAN BUSH, Toronto, Ontario: 1964 graduate; apprentice teacher, The National Ballet School; 1965, teaching privately

DIANNE BUXTON, Toronto, Ontario: 1967 graduate; 1967 to 1969, apprentice teacher, The National Ballet School; 1970, teacher, The National Ballet School

VICKI CARTER, London, Ontario: 1969 graduate; 1969 to 1970, apprentice teacher, The National Ballet School; 1970, teaching in London, Ontario

MARY CLARKSON, Lorne Park, Ontario: 1964 graduate; to grade thirteen

COLLEEN COOL, San Bernadino, California: 1965 graduate; 1965 to 1967, postgraduate student, The National Ballet School, and courses in French and history; 1967 to National Ballet of Canada; now a soloist with that company

ELAINE CRAWFORD, Miami, Florida: 1960 graduate; 1960 to 1961, postgraduate student, The National Ballet School; 1961 to National Ballet of Canada

KAREN CULLINAN, Kenmore, New York: 1969 graduate; 1969 to 1970, postgraduate student, The National Ballet School; 1970 to American Airlines

CHRISTINE CUMBERLAND, Toronto, Ontario: 1968 graduate; 1968 to 1969, postgraduate student, The National Ballet School; 1969 to National Ballet of Canada

CHRISTOPHER CZYZEWSKI, Toronto, Ontario: 1969 graduate; 1969 to 1970, postgraduate student, The National Ballet School, and *Prologue to the Performing Arts; 1970 to National Ballet of Canada

ANDREA DAVIDSON, Toronto, Ontario: 1970 graduate; 1970 to 1971, postgraduate student, The National Ballet School; 1971 to National Ballet of Canada

RICHARD DAVIS, Toronto, Ontario: 1963 graduate; to grade thirteen

ROSALIE DICKS, Thunder Bay, Ontario: 1969 graduate; 1969 to 1971, postgraduate student, The National Ballet School, and *Prologue to the Performing Arts

ANN DITCHBURN, Clarkson, Ontario: 1967 graduate; 1967 to 1968, postgraduate student, The National Ballet School; 1968 to National Ballet of Canada; has choreographed several ballets for that company

DIANE DOBSON, Corona Delmar, California: 1961 graduate; 1961 to 1962, Royal Ballet School, London, England; 1962 to 1963, University of Neuchatel, Switzerland

FRANCES DOBSON, Corona Delmar, California: 1961 graduate; to National Ballet of Canada

CHRISTINE EDINBOROUGH, Toronto, Ontario: 1965 graduate; to grade thirteen; 1966 to 1967, York University, Toronto; to Assistant Stage Manager, Watford Repertory Company, Herts, England

HOPE ELIOT, Ann Arbor, Michigan: 1969 graduate; to Oberlin College, Ohio

MIRANDA ESMONDE, Montreal, Quebec: 1967 graduate; 1966 to 1967, postgraduate student, The National Ballet School; 1967 to 1968, National Ballet of Canada; 1969 to 1970, York University, Toronto

NANCY FERGUSON, Toronto, Ontario: 1969 graduate; 1969 to 1970, postgraduate student, The National Ballet School, and grade thirteen; 1970 to 1971, York University, Toronto

NORMA SUE FISHER, Markham, Ontario: 1970 graduate; 1970 to 1971, postgraduate student, The National Ballet School

LINDA FLETCHER, Buffalo, New York: 1964 graduate; 1964 to 1965, postgraduate student, The National Ballet School; 1965 to National Ballet of Canada; now a soloist with that company

GEORGINA GEDDIS, Toronto, Ontario: 1961 graduate; 1961 to 1962, apprentice teacher, The National Ballet School; 1962 to 1963, teacher, The National Ballet School; 1964 to 1965, to study Benesh Movement Notation, London, England; 1965, teacher, The National Ballet School; 1967 to 1970, teacher and assistant ballet mistress, Royal Swedish Opera Ballet, Stockholm, through arrangement with The National Ballet School

DAVID GORDON, Seattle, Washington: 1967 graduate; 1967 to 1968, postgraduate student, The National Ballet School; 1968 to National Ballet of Canada; 1970 to 1971, Nederlands Dans Theatre, Holland

LEEYAN GRANGER, Buffalo, New York: 1963 graduate; to National Ballet of Canada

ELIZABETH GRAVELLE, Thunder Bay, Ontario: 1970 graduate; 1970 to 1971, postgraduate student, The National Ballet School

JANET HAGEY, Brantford, Ontario: 1965 graduate; to grade thirteen; 1966 to 1967, University of Waterloo

GILLIAN HANNANT, Toronto, Ontario: 1968 graduate; 1968 to 1969 postgraduate student, The National Ballet School; 1969 to 1970, postgraduate student, The National Ballet School, and *Prologue to the Performing Arts; 1970 to National Ballet of Canada

VANESSA HARWOOD, Toronto, Ontario: 1964 graduate; 1964, postgraduate student, The National Ballet School; 1965 to National Ballet of Canada; now a principal dancer with that company

URSULA HAWORTH, Toronto, Ontario: 1963 graduate; to study costume construction

JANE HENDERSON, Delray Beach, Florida: 1966 graduate; 1966 to 1968, apprentice teacher, The National Ballet School; 1968 to 1969, apprentice teacher, Royal Swedish Opera Ballet School, by arrangement with The National Ballet School; 1969 to 1970, teacher, Royal Swedish Opera Ballet School, by arrangement with The National Ballet School

CARLA HUBBARD, Rochester, Minnesota: 1970 graduate; 1970 to 1971, postgraduate student, The National Ballet School

MAKI KABAYAMA, Ottawa, Ontario: 1969 graduate; 1969 to 1970, postgraduate student, The National Ballet School, and *Prologue to the Performing Arts; 1970 to National Ballet of Canada ˙

KAREN KAIN, Erindale, Ontario: 1969 graduate; to National Ballet of Canada; in second year with that company danced Odette/Odile in *Swan Lake*

ELIZABETH KEEBLE, Toronto, Ontario: 1964 graduate; to National Ballet of Canada; now a soloist with Royal Swedish Opera Ballet

JOAN KIRKWOOD, Ottawa, Ontario: 1968 graduate; to Carleton University, Ottawa

SUSAN LAIDLAW, Toronto, Ontario: 1966 graduate; 1966 to 1967, postgraduate student, The National Ballet School; 1967 to National Ballet of Canada

JENNIFER LAIRD, Ottawa, Ontario: 1970 graduate; 1970 to 1971, postgraduate student, The National Ballet School

CAROLE LANDRY, Montreal, Quebec: 1969 graduate; 1969 to 1970, postgraduate student, The National Ballet School, *Prologue to the Performing Arts, and grade thirteen; 1970 to Les Grands Ballets Canadiens, Montreal

Photograph Identification

Jacket   Rehearsal for a lecture-demonstration: Yolanda Sadlowska, Elizabeth Gravelle, Andrea Davidson, Elizabeth Yeigh

End papers   Erik Bruhn and Betty Oliphant with National Ballet School students after class

Opposite title page   Rehearsal for a student performance of Balanchine's *Concerto Barocco*

vi   Susan Embury has her hair arranged in classic style by Joy Boardman

viii   The main building, 111 Maitland Street, Toronto

x   Gillian Hannant and Garry Semeniuk in a performance of Ann Ditchburn's *Listen*

Opposite 1   Veronica Tennant sews ribbons on her shoes during a rehearsal of Celia Franca's *Cinderella*

2   Angela Leigh teaching; Stephanie Leigh with Betty Oliphant

4   Celia Franca rehearses students for their appearance in *Cinderella* with the National Ballet of Canada

6   Left, Tim Spain, David Walker, and Patricia Oney dance at their graduation party; right, Robert Laidlaw with Ann Ditchburn and Patricia Oney

8   Demons versus swans in a student spoof of classical ballet

10   Top, Vincent Bladen, Betty Oliphant, Anna Haworth, and Hilda Bennett applaud a school performance; bottom, Tim Spain earns money for charity the hard way

12   At the barre

14   Students reading Benesh Notation, a precise way of writing down dance movements so the reconstruction of ballets need not rely on the memories of choreographers or ballet masters

16   Podiatrist Peter Walpole treats sore and injured feet during regular visits to the school

18   On the train, for a *Nutcracker* performance in Montreal

20   Top, wating to check into the hotel on arrival; bottom, card games help pass travel time for Andrea Davidson, David Gordon, and Tim Spain

22   Arriving for a performance at Place des Arts, Montreal

23   Homework in residence

24   End of a pillow fight

26   Robert Desrosiers, Trevor Smallwood, and Frank Augustyn try the parallel bars during a special gym class at Jarvis Collegiate

28   Carole Chadwick teaching

30   Karen Bowes and Hazaros Surmeyan in John Cranko's *Romeo and Juliet* with the National Ballet of Canada

31   Karen Bowes in class with Daniel Seillier

32   The lunchroom for day students, with murals painted by the art class

34   Betty Oliphant (top) talks with students before an end-of-the-year demonstration class and (bottom) teaches summer school.

36   Limbering exercises

38   Watching a summer school class from the main building's front door

40   A weekend picnic during summer school—food, games, and swimming

42   Creative dance class

44   Stretching exercise: Tim Spain, Brian Silversides

46   Summer school class with Carole Chadwick

48   Tim Spain rehearses his first ballet, with David Walker, Karen Kain, Barry Smith, Garry Semeniuk, Miranda Esmonde, and Colleen Cool (seated)

50   Performance of a student ballet, with Ann Ditchburn, Barry Smith, Miranda Esmonde, Jane Mogg, and David Walker

52   The girls' dressing room

53 Backstage during *Nutcracker:* Karen Bowes, Murray Kilgour, Nadia Potts, and some of Mother Gigogne's Clowns (Lois Boardman at the right) watch a performance from the wings

54 James Kudelka making up for *Nutcracker*

56 Warming up before an end-of-the-year demonstration class for parents and friends

58 Nadia Potts, Erik Bruhn, and Yves Cousineau in the National Ballet of Canada production of *La Sylphide*

60 During an engagement in Toronto, Erik Bruhn takes time to watch a class (with National Ballet Company ballet master David Scott) as Betty Oliphant teaches

62 Nancy Schwenker Kilgour teaches a class in character dance

64 Betty Oliphant and Wendy Reiser (in black leotard) with students of the Royal Swedish Ballet School in Stockholm

65 Betty Oliphant and Wendy Reiser visit with Rudolph Nureyev after a performance of *Swan Lake* in Stockholm

66 Pas de deux class: Daniel Seillier, Gillian Hannant, and Ian Amos

68 Pas de deux class

69 Daniel Seillier with Karen Kain and Tim Spain; Karen Kain and Tim Spain

70 Stretching exercise: Susan Embury and Gloria Luoma

72 Yoga class

74 In the school library

76 The art class paints a mural

78 Between classes

80 Top, Lucy Potts teaching; bottom, study period: Sonia Perusse and Michelle Jory

82 Pas de deux class: Veronica Tennant, Earl Kraul, and Daniel Seillier watched by Karen Kain, Gillian Hannant, Christopher Bannerman

84 Students take part in a CBC-TV variety special with Don Gillies: Deborah Castellan, Debra Gellman, Elizabeth Gravelle, Wendy Reiser and Andrea Davidson

86 Sand sculpture on a summer picnic

90 Creative dance class

94 The senior girls' residence

98 At the barre

This book was printed in Canada by Herzig Somerville Limited
Typesetting: Fast Typesetters of Canada Limited
Type face: Bembo Roman and Bembo Italic
Paper: Imperial Offset Enamel 100 lb.
Cloth: Millbank Linen 974
Binder: John Deyell Limited
Photographs reproduced by duotone black and grey
from prints made by Peter Varley
Book design: Miriam Bloom